JAMES HULL &
BEDE BRENNAN

SHIT GARDENS

**IMPRESSIVELY
UNCONVENTIONAL
LANDSCAPING**

Published and distributed by Knock Knock
1635 Electric Ave.
Venice, CA 90291
knockknockstuff.com
Knock Knock is a registered trademark of Knock Knock LLC

© 2018 James Hull and Bede Brennan
All rights reserved
Printed in China

No part of this product may be used or reproduced in any manner whatsoever without prior written permission from the publisher, except in the case of brief quotations embodied in critical articles and reviews. For information, address Knock Knock.

This book is meant solely for entertainment purposes. The designation of a garden as "shit" is purely an expression of opinion. In no event will Knock Knock be liable to any reader for any harm, injury, or damages, including direct, indirect, incidental, special, consequential, or punitive arising out of or in connection with the use of the information contained in this book. So there.

Where specific company, product, and brand names are cited, copyright and trademarks associated with these names are the property of their respective owners. Every reasonable attempt has been made to identify owners of copyright. Errors or omissions will be corrected in subsequent editions.

ISBN: 978-168349054-8
UPC: 825703502398

10 9 8 7 6 5 4 3 2 1

5	INTRODUCTION
7	**TOPIARIES**» 100% Plant-Based Surrealism
25	**GARDENS OF ANTIQUITY**» Sentimental Statuary
43	**ASTROTURF**» The Future of Lawn
57	**HARD SURFACES**» High-Performance Concrete
71	**WATER FEATURES**» From Atlantis to the Present
89	**ZEN GARDENS**» The Suburban Minimalist
105	**WTF**» Rethinking the Absurd

INTRODUCTION

Everyone knows a shit garden. Everyone's neighborhood has at least one. In an age of overly perfected, mass-produced gardens, sometimes it's the shit ones that stick out, the ones that evoke a sense of mystery through their curiousness and peculiarity. The idea of *Shit Gardens* in itself came about from long walks through suburbia, where we would find gardens that seemed inexplicably bad, and began to wonder just how they came about. We gradually came to appreciate these sorts of gardens and the way they so effortlessly juxtaposed the grand ambitions of intent with the inelegance of unfinished reality.

In terms of composition, the notion of what constitutes a shit garden is something that has evolved greatly over the years, and although there is a tendency toward shit gardens evolving in line with gardening trends, there are also those gardens that buck the idea of trends completely—true mavericks in their own right.

When it comes to shit gardens, there's a big difference between gardens that have become shit as a result of neglect and ambivalence and gardens that are shit on the basis of a wayward approach to design. What interests us most are those gardens that display the latter, with a misunderstanding of scale, an appreciation for the weird, or a bold disregard for convention. At the end of the day, we're all about equilibrium and balance. You can't appreciate the good without recognizing the bad.

From triumphant topiaries to expansive uses of astroturf, there is truly no horticultural format that a shit garden cannot touch. Come join us for a chapter-by-chapter account of all things *Shit Gardens*, as we peer in search of hidden gems that have come to shape and—in an oddly endearing way—enhance the suburban terrain.

—*James Hull & Bede Brennan*

TOPIARIES
100% PLANT-BASED SURREALISM

Topiary is the art of sculpting a plant into the shape of something that isn't a plant. Why people embark upon this exceedingly laborious task is something we're still quite unsure of. Ranging from exquisitely executed animate-objects (cats and dogs are our favorites) to poorly trimmed blobs and orbs (often these appear in groups), the topiary can take on many different forms.

Aside from their versatility, topiaries—we observed—have an astounding ability to self-seed into the gardens of one's neighbors. This is something we came to notice during our long outer-suburban pilgrimages, where we would walk onto quiet streets in search of topiaries, only to find that the entire street had been mysteriously overcome by them. After carefully studying this phenomenon, we began developing theories to explain these congregations of suburban topiaries.

Our favorite theory of the topiary was one that posited a type of "topiary jealousy," in which "keeping up with the Joneses" becomes a high priority in an ever-escalating sense of neighborhood competition. Another theory we explored was that some sort of collective topiary mania was taking over the streets, much like the unexplained "tulip mania" of seventeenth-century Holland, where whole streets became adorned with this triffid-like phenomenon. To us, these topiarous avenues of tortured plant-forms have a surreal and inexplicably charming quality.

Carefully curated creatures provide a substitute for pets

On-street parking

King of the jungle

Erect army of topiaries stand tall

Reserved space:
power dress your garden

Ficus benjamina shows subtle disregard for parking restrictions

Existential shrub:
Sisyphus awaits

Diamond-four-seven:
a numerical display

Reds under the railing:
an encroaching Eastern star

Cunning eyes and clicking grin

Pruning plateau:
nature's limitation

our ad here

Talking heads

Tapping into the suburban vernacular

Legs/Eleven

TOPIARIES
THE MANY FACES OF AMATEUR HEDGING

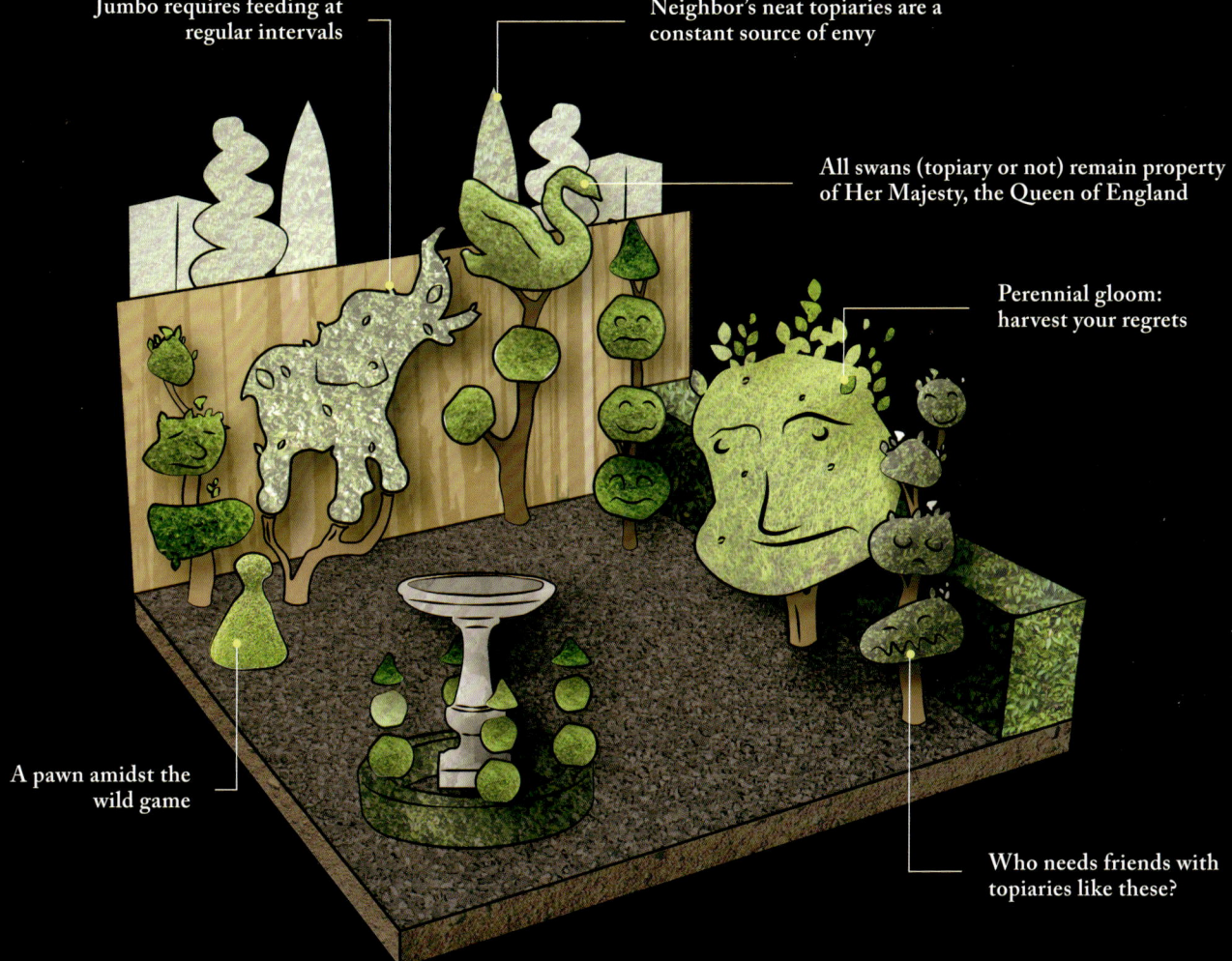

GARDENS OF ANTIQUITY
SENTIMENTAL STATUARY

Statues and sculptures in the garden come in all shapes and sizes. From the tallest reproduction of Michelangelo's *David* to the smallest Virgin Mother, the historic, patriotic, religious, totemistic, and just plain bizarre are all at home in the garden.

The idea of building historical monuments in public gardens is almost as old as the idea of a public garden itself. The placement of these monuments in your neighbor's yard, however, is something you wouldn't have seen until much more recently. While there are many different ways in which statues and historical icons can feature in the garden, our favorites are generally the bolder examples, which tend to be of the Greek or Roman persuasion.

As powerful figures yearn for redemption against a backdrop of decaying shrubbery, one can't help but feel a sense of betrayal when looking at the way these once-great kings and queens have been reduced to superfluous effigies of moss and mire. Yet still, people take pride in the erection of these images, often associating an air of distinction with even the most whimsical display of neoclassical pageantry. But is this really the case? What's so great about having a statue of an ancient ruler or philosopher standing in your yard? And lastly, does that neoclassical bust jutting out from the front of your house really give you cultural capital over the neighbor who stuck with garden gnomes? We should think not.

Homo erectus

The makings of a strange narrative

A tender moment:
woman by the well

Alert Trojan:
the cunning member and his Doric pillar

Fountains of hoof:
bursting forth with virility

Swan fake

Size matters:
Michelangelo's *David* revisited

Ornamental miscellany

Pride rock

Visions of grandeur

A sense of porpoise

Our lady of the Toyota Camry

Atlantis now:
a chalice to the gods

Suburban soliloquy:
a far cry from Rome

All things tend toward their ruin

legendary sea creature

Sunbathing siren:
bold but beautiful

t fountain:
s wasn't in the brochure

Slow decay:
an ode to rubble

GARDENS OF ANTIQUITY

A PICK'N'MIX FOR THE DISCERNING GARDEN HISTORIAN

41

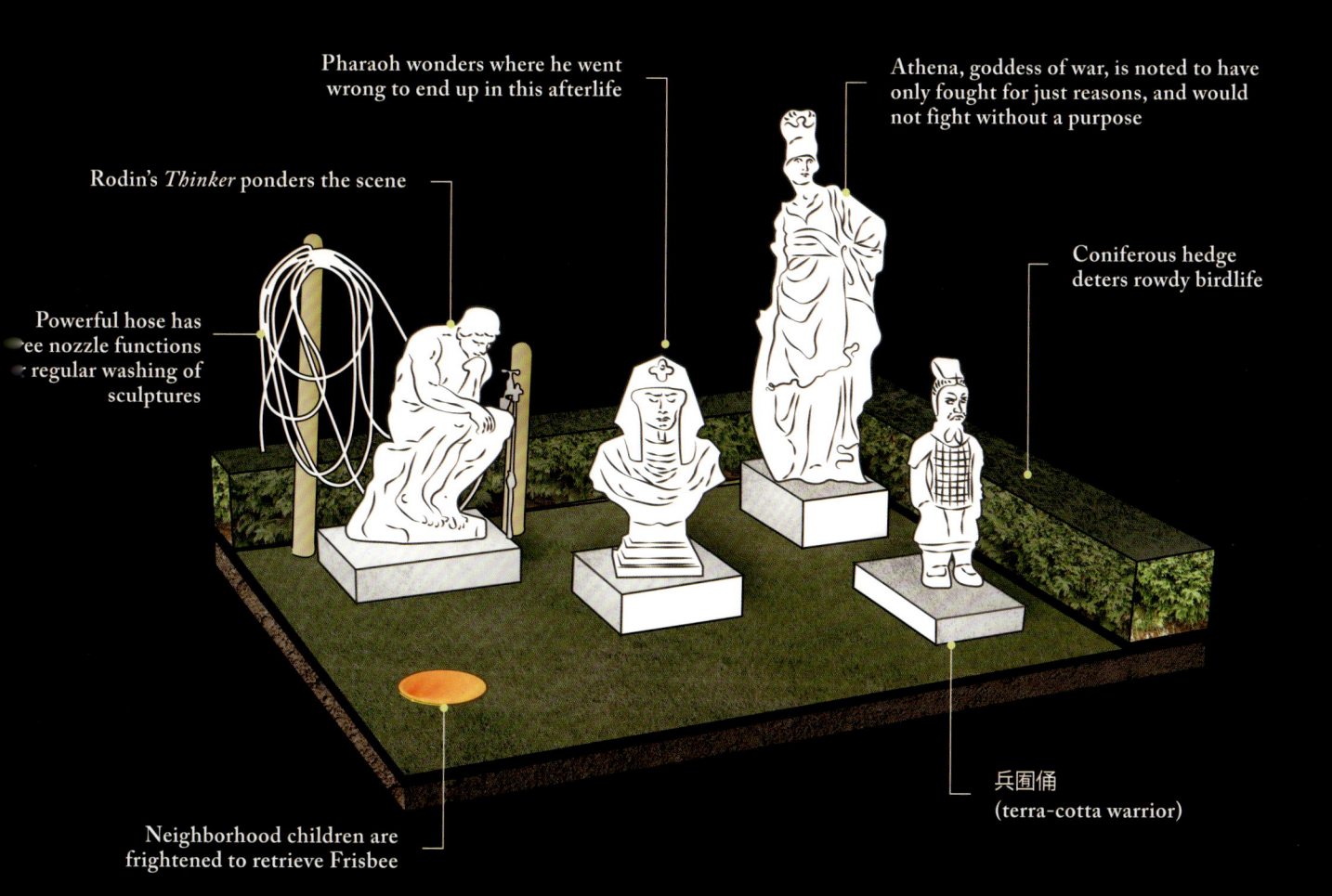

Rodin's *Thinker* ponders the scene

Pharaoh wonders where he went wrong to end up in this afterlife

Athena, goddess of war, is noted to have only fought for just reasons, and would not fight without a purpose

Powerful hose has ee nozzle functions regular washing of sculptures

Coniferous hedge deters rowdy birdlife

Neighborhood children are frightened to retrieve Frisbee

兵囲俑
(terra-cotta warrior)

ASTROTURF
THE FUTURE OF LAWN

As the name suggests, astroturf was developed by NASA for use on the moon.* However, unlike dehydrated space-food, which has struggled to take off on Earth, astroturf has managed to find numerous earthy applications. Whether it be for the contrived look of a run-down bohemian bar or for the surroundings of a concrete fountain, when it comes to astroturf, nothing is sacred.

Despite concerns around toxicity, environmental damage, longevity, and its obvious tackiness, the future looks bright for astroturf, with global sales on the rise. Why people cover their gardens (and other objects) in plastic mock-grass continues to intrigue and bemuse us so much that we made a list of the things we've seen covered in astroturf: Tables, chairs, various vehicles, a leather suitcase, jackets, a bicycle seat, prams, pencil cases, shoes, books, a ceiling, a cap, a chessboard, a car seat, a laptop cover, a man's head, a flower vase, and more.

As our list would imply, the uses for astroturf are endless. It is a highly versatile medium that flourishes both visually and practically, regardless of context. Yet it will always be the suburban garden that fosters the true home of astroturf.

*not true

AstroTree™

Fact—there are more plastic flamingos in the world than there are real ones

Green expanses:
an added dimension

Water meter feature

All synthetic paths lead to one

Fabricated fanfare

Polka-dot pathways:
the day has just begun

Verdant Zone

The Hanging Gardens of Babylon is the only wonder of
the ancient world whose location has not been established

Artificial intelligence

Ornamental drain

Turf medley:
variety is best

The automobile industry embraces green innovation

ASTROTURF
FAUX PAS OR FAUX GRASS?

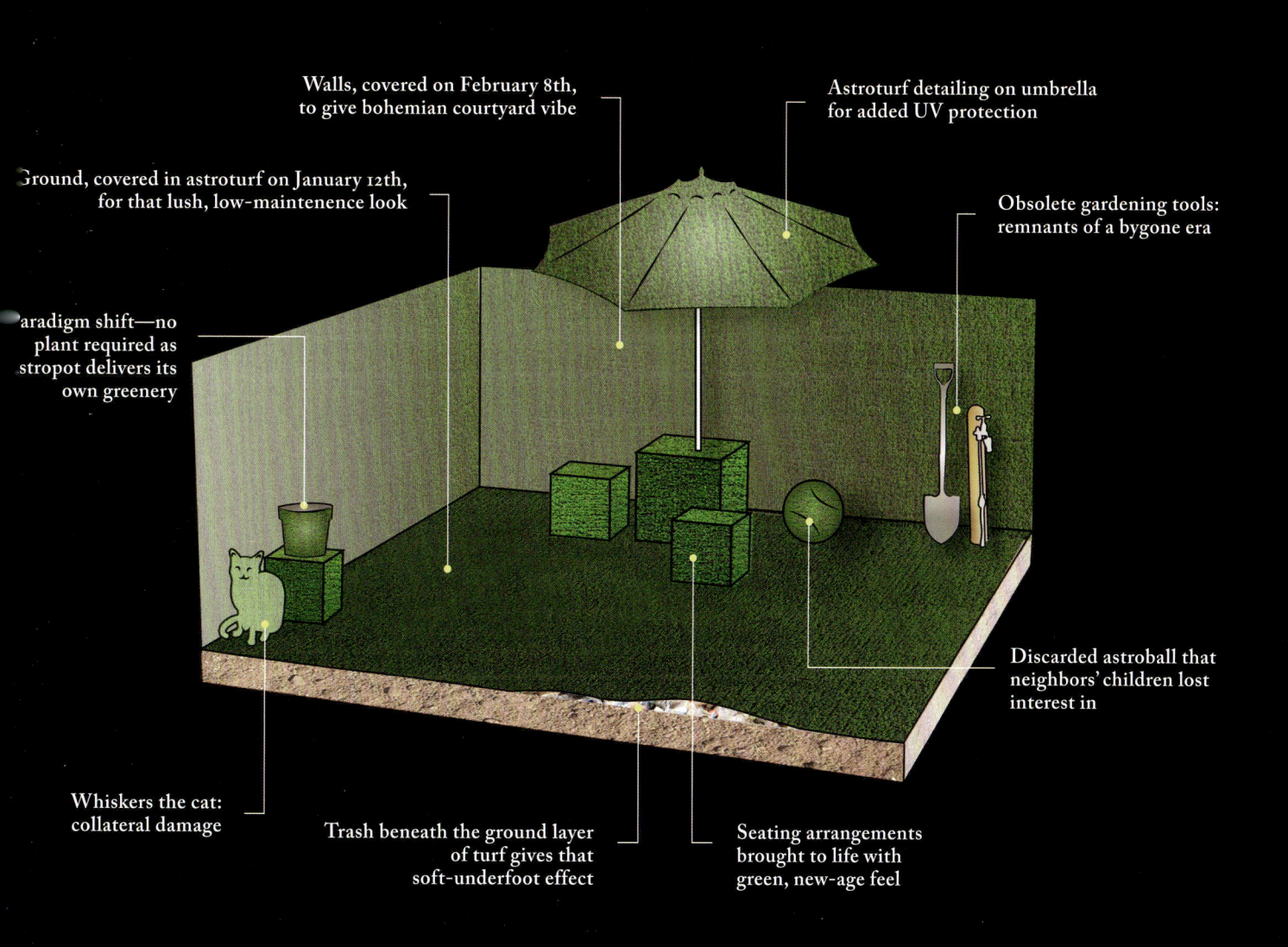

Walls, covered on February 8th, to give bohemian courtyard vibe

Astroturf detailing on umbrella for added UV protection

Ground, covered in astroturf on January 12th, for that lush, low-maintenance look

Obsolete gardening tools: remnants of a bygone era

Paradigm shift—no plant required as astropot delivers its own greenery

Discarded astroball that neighbors' children lost interest in

Whiskers the cat: collateral damage

Trash beneath the ground layer of turf gives that soft-underfoot effect

Seating arrangements brought to life with green, new-age feel

HARD SURFACES
HIGH-PERFORMANCE CONCRETE

It may come as a surprise to you too, but sometimes the factors that contribute toward creating shit gardens have very little to do with gardening at all. Sometimes they have more to do with the everyday dilemmas we face as humans, such as *"where the fuck am I going to park my car!?"* With the proliferation of the motor vehicle over the past half century, people are running out of parking spots almost as quickly as they've run out of creative uses for their gardens, making the allure of a paved-over front yard more appealing than ever.

Popular alternatives to the tried-and-true method of grass and shrub include radioactive gravel, colored mulch, high-performance concrete, and various tessellating patterns of paving.

Though commonly horizontal in appearance, the hard surface can take on all sorts of unique forms from tiered levels to brutalist pebble-crete structures and cement facades. The reasons behind these choices in design are not always immediately obvious. However, the minimization of maintenance and a general distrust of the temperamental nature of plant-life are popular motives. Thus, while a plant might disappoint by dropping its leaves, an expanse or object made from high-performance concrete can always be relied upon.

Concrete material, aquatic themes

59

Creative drought strikes again

concrete pride

Strange orbit:
martian's landing

Mixed-terrain tiling solution

Alms for the poor

Man's best friend

Bleak house:
an all-too-familiar fountain

The lone diamond's solitary plight

Creature feature

HARD SURFACES
TYPICAL DESIGN FEATURES ASPIRED TO BY MANY "LOW-MAINTENANCE" HOME GARDENERS

69

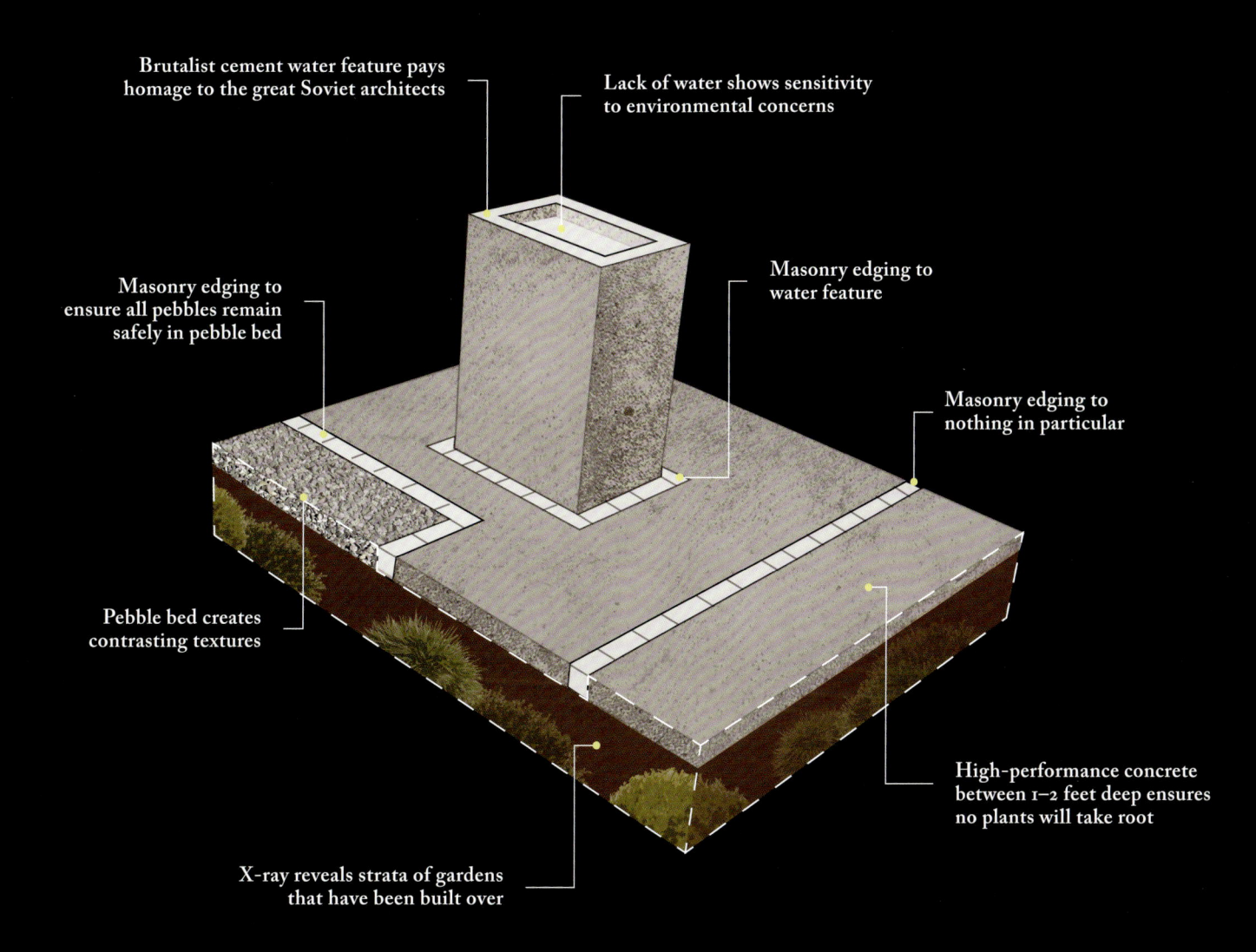

Brutalist cement water feature pays homage to the great Soviet architects

Lack of water shows sensitivity to environmental concerns

Masonry edging to ensure all pebbles remain safely in pebble bed

Masonry edging to water feature

Masonry edging to nothing in particular

Pebble bed creates contrasting textures

High-performance concrete between 1–2 feet deep ensures no plants will take root

X-ray reveals strata of gardens that have been built over

WATER FEATURES
FROM ATLANTIS TO THE PRESENT

With humble origins, the relationship between gardens and water features is one that has truly stood the test of time. Although the typical suburban water feature might be a far cry from what you'd expect to see in Rome or Versailles, it's safe to say that each suburban water feature is special in its own little way.

With the West's embrace of feng shui, a system of beliefs that places emphasis on the flow of running water, it is no surprise that water features have shot up in popularity over recent years. However, in saying this, suburban water features that lose water at a faster rate than they are filled up (the vast majority) offer no benefit to one's pursuit of enlightenment and can be seen as tokenistic at best.

From daring attempts at Chinese minimalism to the uninspiring accolades of ancient Rome and Napoleonic France, the suburban water feature can take on almost any form. Some, on the other hand, veer away from the traditional template of historical homage, acting instead as places of refuge and refreshment for birds and wildlife. Although running water is appealing to creatures of all shapes and sizes, most suburban water features, as a result of neglect, are overcome by moss and algae, and tend to scare these creatures away.

A month of Sundays

Fountain of misogyny:
dying art

Lady in waiting:
Venus and her hose-pipe

Urban ecology:
an odd remnant

Suburban swimmer:
the unlikely Olympian

Brutalist water feature

Blossoming brickwork

Aviary's foreclosure:
desire to bathe denied

Soviet monument fosters elegant birdlife

The potter's pelicans:
how many do you see?

Urban oasis

Flipper-clad lantern adorns a fountain form

nphitrite, goddess of the ocean:
ninished by poets, bound to the sea

Eau de toilette

Demos kratis:
an Athenian legacy

Janus birdbath:
always looking on

Ochre gravel surrounds monochrome pageantry

WATER FEATURES
FROM NEPTUNE TO POSEIDON, IN A SUBURB NEAR YOU

87

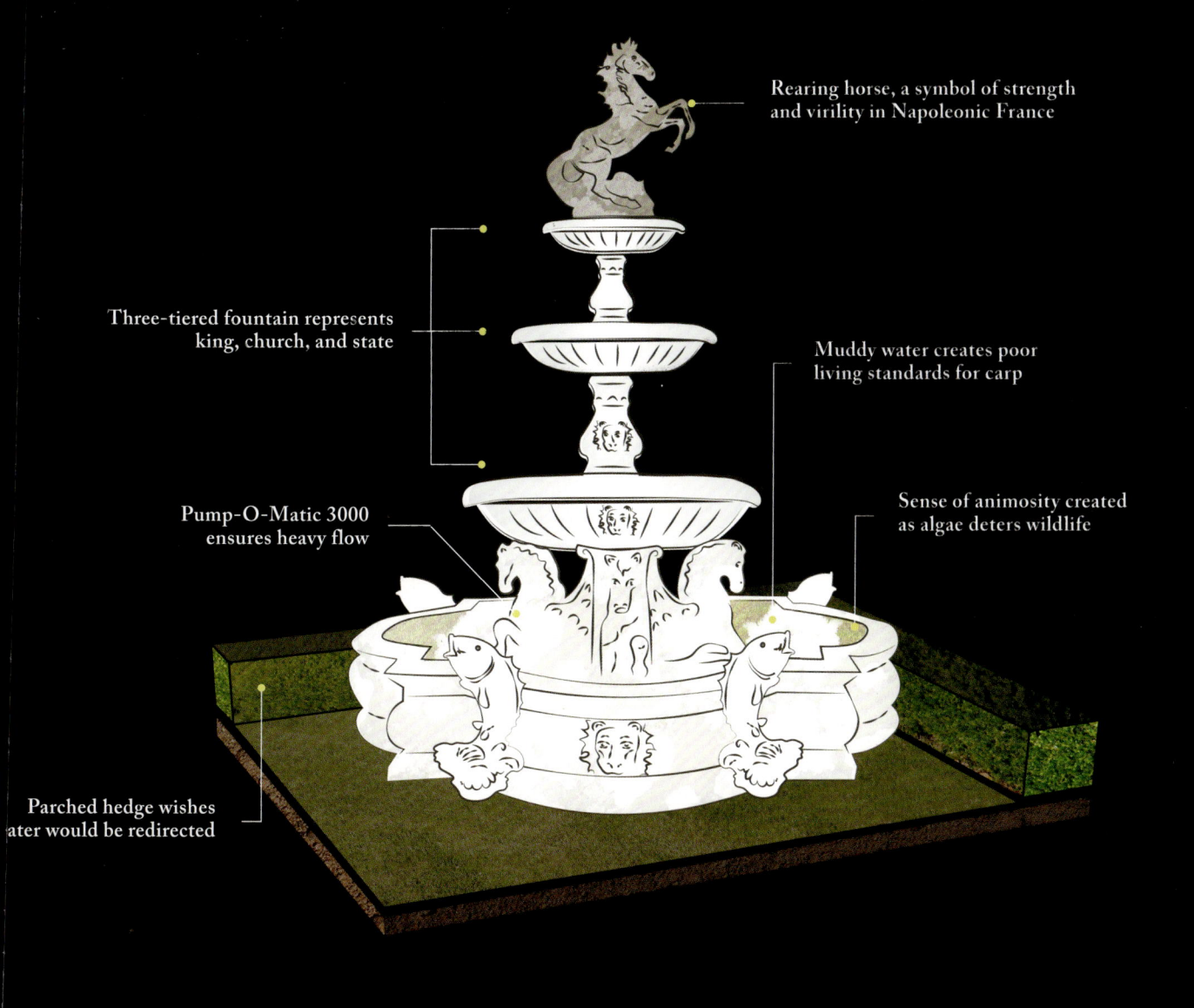

Rearing horse, a symbol of strength and virility in Napoleonic France

Three-tiered fountain represents king, church, and state

Muddy water creates poor living standards for carp

Pump-O-Matic 3000 ensures heavy flow

Sense of animosity created as algae deters wildlife

Parched hedge wishes water would be redirected

ZEN GARDENS
THE SUBURBAN MINIMALIST

Some of the most elegant and beautiful gardens in the world are the manicured Zen gardens of Japanese temples. But by the same token, some of the most exemplary shit gardens also fit into this category. Although the intent of the owner may have been to encapsulate the "less is more" ethos that makes Japanese landscaping so unique and interesting, often these attempts result in a rather different representation of the Zen ethos, with vast expanses of gravel and bridges leading to nowhere.

A more obvious stab at the Zen tradition, and one that perhaps appears more prominently, is the random placement of Buddhas in and around the garden. Generally speaking, these crudely fashioned deities are in fact carvings of Buddhas that appear in major temples around the world. Although they all seem quite similar, if you look carefully, you will notice that each individual statue comes with its own unique hand-gesture or pose.

While some of these hand-gestures typify symbols of unity and harmony, others merely serve as reminders of the value of serenity. Although these gestures all symbolize different things, there is one thing that Buddha statues share in common—a strong sense of belief that suburban Zen is here to stay.

Dharma and the drainpipe

Shit ceremony

Suburban soliloquy

A balanced approach: symmetry of the mind

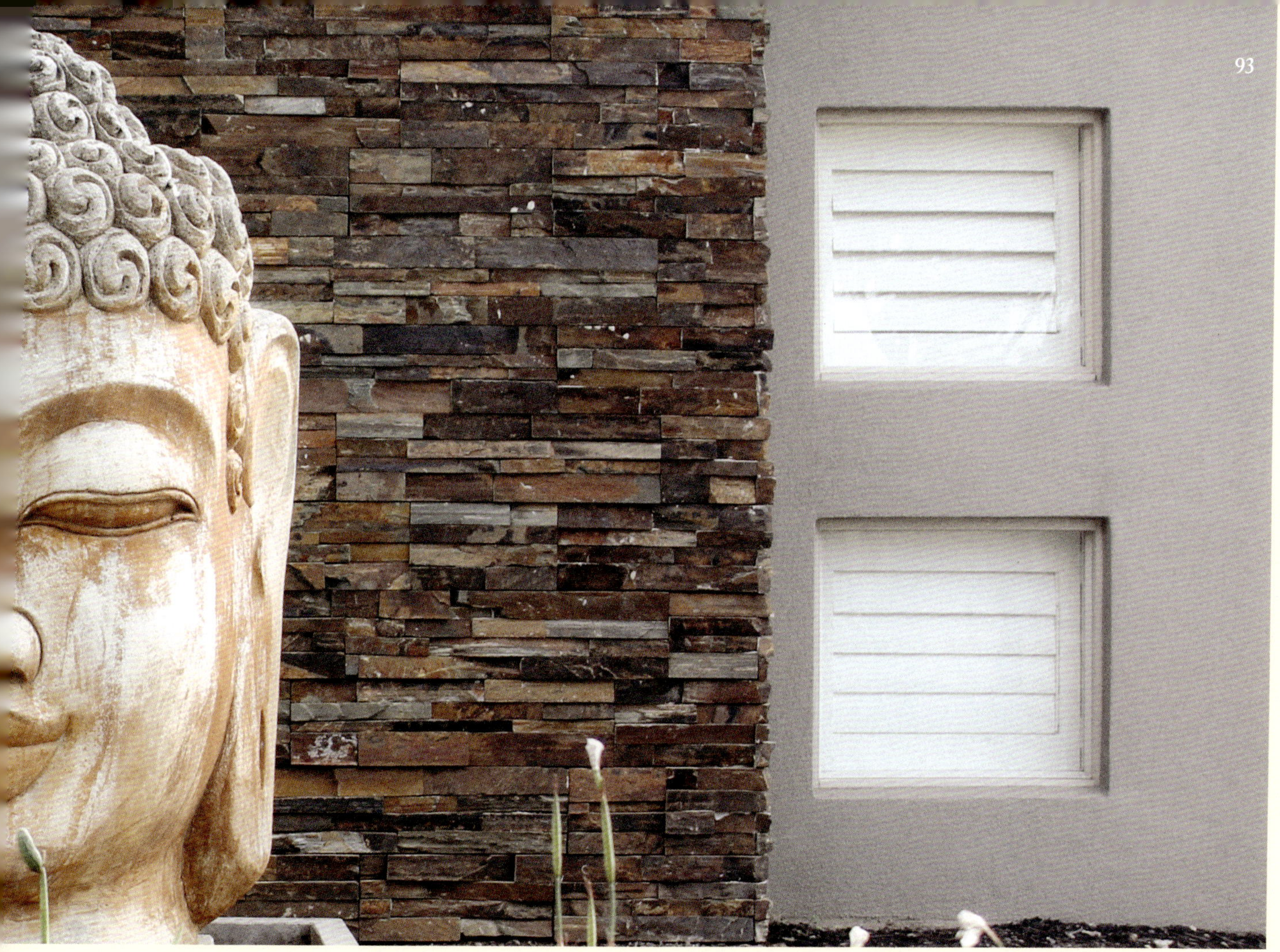

Post-impressionist:
primary colors

Reclining Buddha:
the dozing deity

Buddha of the 'burbs:
noble eightfold path to urban sprawl

Outback Buddha

Koan:
what is a bridge without water?

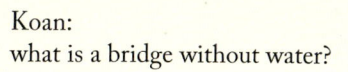

Suburban enlightenment:
Buddhas look within

Golden Buddha:
protectorate against bad omens and junk mail

Manifest your desire with a two-car garage

East meets West

Buddha's budgies

Aqua profunda:
a sense of wonder

SUBURBAN ZEN

FEATURES AVAILABLE AT ANY DISCOUNT NURSERY OR POT WAREHOUSE

103

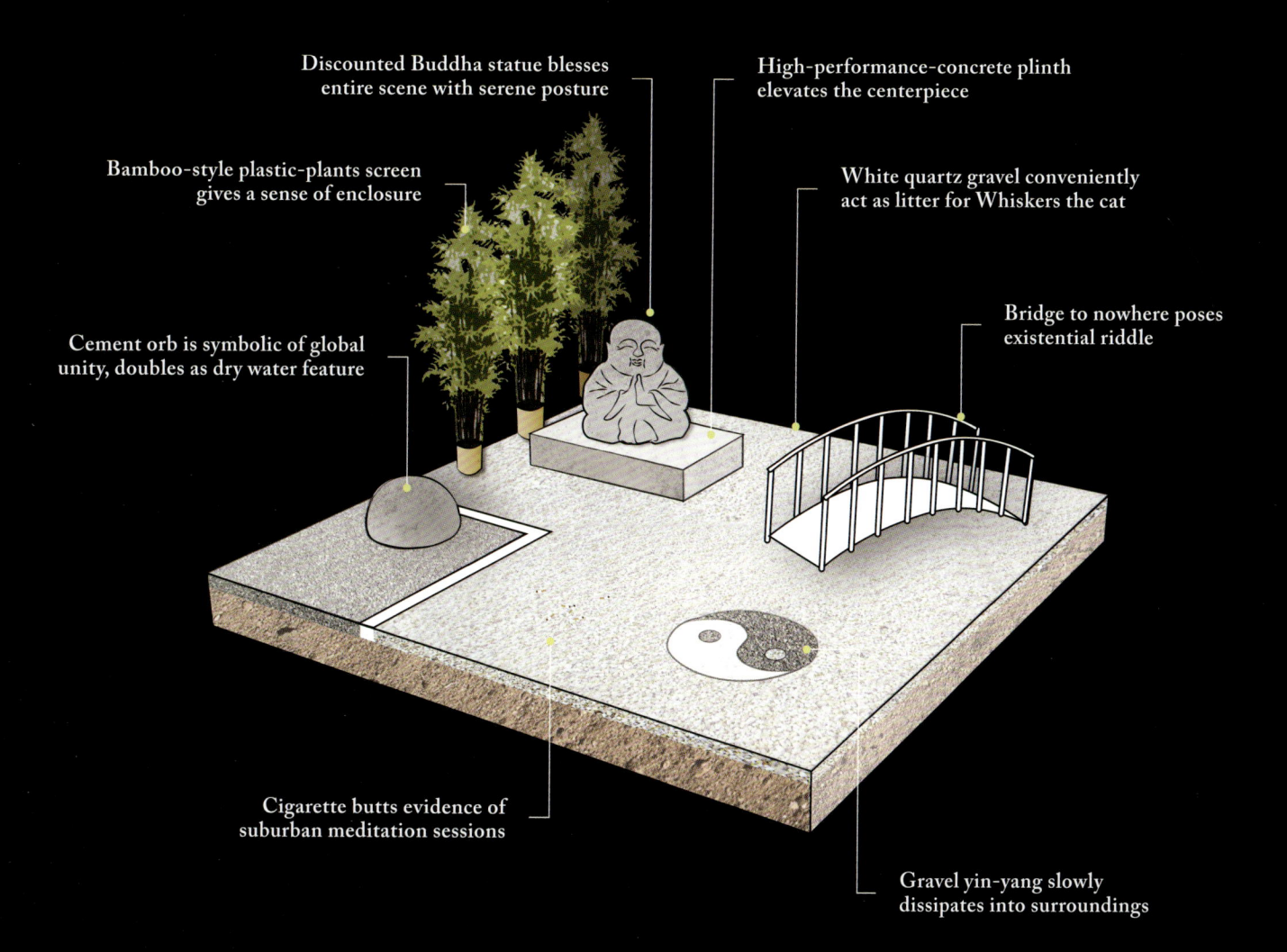

Discounted Buddha statue blesses entire scene with serene posture

High-performance-concrete plinth elevates the centerpiece

Bamboo-style plastic-plants screen gives a sense of enclosure

White quartz gravel conveniently act as litter for Whiskers the cat

Cement orb is symbolic of global unity, doubles as dry water feature

Bridge to nowhere poses existential riddle

Cigarette butts evidence of suburban meditation sessions

Gravel yin-yang slowly dissipates into surroundings

WTF
RETHINKING THE ABSURD

As we mentioned in our introduction, when it comes to shit gardens, there's a big difference between gardens that have become shit through neglect and carelessness, and gardens that are shit on the basis of a considered and well-thought-out approach that makes absolutely no sense. It is the latter that tend to be the most interesting shit gardens, the ones that cause you to turn your head and look a second time, or maybe even a third, and ask yourself, **"What. The. Fuck."**

It's these inexplicably strange gardens, the gardens that transcend the notion of being categorically bad, that often end up being our favorites. While most shit gardens have found their way into this book on the merit of having featured strange statues, weird water features, or pitiful pavers, there are some that simply cannot be categorized. In much the same way, they can't really be explained either. The only real way to conjure up worthy descriptions of these gardens that defy all the senses is to provide visual examples.

Building bridges to overcome the
unnecessary obstacles in our lives

Muffin-top yuccas

Art student 101

Desire lines:
linear movement denied

Genghis Khan and his green thumb

Post-orifice

Every rose has its thorn

III

My neighbor, Totoro

The lion, the kitsch, and the awkward

Sensory overload:
a romantic liaison

Caught between a rock and a hard place

Handy man

Soul-less

115

Paths to serenity:
the postman's choice

opical fruit

Graduates of the garden

Chernobyl cherub:
a poignant reminder of nuclear consequence

Evocative sculpture

Suppressed cupressus

Since the Romans first brewed wine, humans have been suffering hangovers

oo stoned

Cactus Jack

122

Mobile kitchen garden

The grass between your toes

That sinking feeling

Perennial Christmas

Gnome focus

ABOUT THE AUTHORS

———

Bede and James have known each other since bonding over a mutual dislike of their eighth-grade mathematics teacher. Funnily enough, James is now a teacher himself, while Bede, on the other hand, is a landscape architect. Together, they are *Shit Gardens*.

ACKNOWLEDGMENTS

———

Thanks to the friends and family who put up with us while we wrote this book, and a big thank you to everyone who assisted us by sending in images. Without your help this would not have been possible. But most of all, thanks to all the crazy gardeners out there who keep the suburbs interesting.

PHOTO CREDITS

Peter Adley: 45 L, 62

Greg Areas: 64

Robert Ashton: 49

Kasey Bromee: 114

Leigh Buchanan: 109 L

Dashiel Carty: 58-59

Robbie Dixon: 99

Scott Dooley: 63

Naomi Drage: 128

Auldmate Durrie: 113

Nikita Ferguson: 76

Philip Grapes: 65 R

Lindsay Gutteridge: 106 L

Owen Harris: 96

Jo Chong Wa: 9

Liz Jones: 10-11, 19, 31 L, 32, 61, 67 L, 72, 125

Peter Lacki: 20

Constance Leonard: 122

Luke Murphy-Gregory: 26 L

Kusum Normoyle: 123 L

Sammii O'Rourke: 124

Crystal Prigmore: 117 R

Cathryn Prowse: 16-17

Helen Singer: 13

Michelle Smith: 119 L

Sarah Sprontos: 37

Scott Waterhouse: 115 L

Dean West: 81 L

Corey Wilson: 12 R

Andrew Zanette: 53, 115 R, 120, 121 L, 121 R

A traumatic scene at the garden depot